Dear Parents and Educators,

Welcome to *Bea is for Business*™, an innovative, educational platform dedicated to teaching young people about business. We believe strongly that business education needs to start early at school and at home. And this book is just the beginning. There's also a website, **www.beaisforbusiness.com**, where you and your child can delve deeper into a variety of business topics, vocabulary, classroom curriculums, focus groups, and do-at-home activities.

All the activities and opportunities included in the *Bea is for Business* educational platform are built off the Common Core State Standards and aim to do the following:

- Help teach basic business principles and monetary concepts

- Expand business vocabulary and language

- Create learning opportunities for kids to think differently and solve problems creatively

- Foster an environment of feedback and encouragement

- Inspire kids to be entrepreneurs as they conceive or implement business ideas

At the end of the book, your child is encouraged to write to Bea via the website with any business ideas he or she may have. Parents, that's where you come in. Please sit down with your child, talk through ideas, and submit a business idea together. Bea can serve as a consultant for your child's business idea. We hope to hear from you. More importantly though, we hope this begins a new learning journey that inspires the next generation of entrepreneurs.

All the best,

Jamie A. Brown & Meg Seitz

To JT. And IT & ET - Here's to all the businesses you'll dream of. J.B.

To Mom, Daddy, & Maret; hugs and kisses to the moon. To S.H., with love. M.S.

For Carter & Sydney, K.L.

Published by:

Bea is for Business, LLC, P.O. Box 3009, Charlotte, NC 28230

For more information and educational resources, please visit: www.beaisforbusiness.com

ISBN 978-0-9893403-0-4 (pbk) - ISBN 978-0-9893403-1-1 (ebook)

First Edition 2013

Bea is for Business

By Jamie A. Brown and Meg Seitz
Illustrated By Karen Lee

Addy —
Happy Birthday
Sweet girl!

"Jackpot!" I shout. "I did it myself!"

I strung a new soccer ball charm on my bracelet. Grandpa sent it to me last week for my birthday. He bought it in Europe.

The phone rings. My bracelet jingles as I slide into the kitchen.

"Hello, Banks' residence.
Miss Beatrice Banks speaking."

"Bea, it's me, Lander."

Lander is my best friend. He has a cool middle name—Lincoln. His parents named him after President Abraham Lincoln.

"What are you up to?" Lander asks.

"Refueling from soccer," I say. "What's new?"

"My mom's wildflowers are in full bloom. She told me to do something creative with them," Lander says. "Want to come over and help me?"

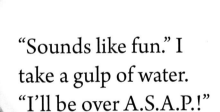

"Sounds like fun." I take a gulp of water. "I'll be over A.S.A.P.!"

I pedal down Commerce Street to Lander's house. My dog, Hamilton, jogs beside me.

I park in Lander's driveway. Hamilton and I run around to the backyard.

"Look at all these beautiful flowers!" I shout.

"What do you think we should do with them?" asks Lander.

Tapping the toe of my shoe, I brainstorm. I think of a few things we could do with these flowers.

Then, I have the best idea ever!

"I've got it!" I exclaim. "Let's pick the flowers, and make them into bouquets."

We open the screen door and walk into the kitchen.

"What's a bouquet?" asks Lander.

"People buy them from flower shops and grocery stores," I reply. "They're all sorts of flowers bundled together for one price. I'll show you. Do you have a napkin and a pen, Lander?"

Lander hands me a clean napkin and a pen. I draw my idea on the napkin.

"Oh, I know what they are," he says, nodding. "Dad brings one home to Mom sometimes."

"We can pick the flowers and tie them together with ribbon," I say. "Then, we can sell them."

"We can sell them at the Storey Farm
Festival this weekend!" Lander adds.

"Jackpot!" I shout. "That's good thinking.
All we need is ribbon!"

Lander's dad helps us find ribbon.
We pick the flowers. We cut the ribbon.
Then, the three of us sit down in the grass with
piles of wildflowers arranged in front of us.

"I'll start a bouquet with red and white flowers,"
I say. "Then, I will pass the bouquet to Lander.
He will add the orange and purple flowers."

"Then, I'll hand the flowers to my dad,"
continues Lander. "He'll add the yellow flowers,
and tie them with ribbon."

"It's like an assembly line!" I exclaim. "It saves
time, and all the bouquets will look alike!"

We get to work.
In no time, we make 20 beautiful bouquets.

After we clean up, Lander and I lie in the grass to count clouds.

"How much should we charge for each bouquet?" asks Lander.

"Maybe $5 each," I reply.

"Hey, Dad!" Lander yells. "How much money would you pay for a bouquet?"

"Maybe $5," Lander's dad answers.

President Lincoln is on the $5 bill—
and Lincoln is Lander's middle name.

"Makes sense," Lander says, smiling.

"Dollars and sense," I giggle.

Saturday arrives. Today, Lander and I will sell our home-made bouquets at the Storey Farm Festival.

I am over-the-moon excited that my mom is coming with us. Mom runs her own business.

Think of yourself as on the threshold of unparalleled success. A whole, clear, glorious life lies before you. Achieve! Achieve!

Andrew Carnegie

Local Fresh Flowers for sale! $5

We stop at Lander's house.

"You ready, Lander?" I shout.

Lander emerges from the backyard pulling his wagon full of bouquets. Mom calls all the bouquets our "inventory."

"I'm ready!" Lander hollers back. "Let's roll!"

Before we enter the festival, I look around.

I see food trucks, families, and kids
with painted faces.

No one is selling flowers. I feel worried.
I've never sold anything before.

What if this doesn't work?

I take one big, deep breath.

I step forward through the festival entrance.

"Well, well, well... look who it is," I hear someone say. I feel a knot in my stomach.

It's Nigel DeFault. He's riding his new, super-fast, black scooter. We call that scooter Black Friday.

"Hi, Nigel," I say. I try to be nice to Nigel. It's not easy because he is mean sometimes.

"What are you doing with those flowers?" Nigel asks. He leans over Black Friday's handlebars to examine Lander's wagon.

"We're selling them!" Lander says excitedly.

"Why would people want to buy your silly flowers?" Nigel chuckles as he rocks back and forth.

I stare at Nigel. He stares right back. I'm brainstorming a good answer. My mind busily races, and then...

"They're beautiful and locally grown!" I say, smiling. "And we're the only ones selling flowers. There's no competition, so we can make money!"

Nigel grumbles under his breath. Then, he rolls his eyes and scoots away.

Lander and I run to catch up with my mom.

"Where do you think the most people will see your bouquets?" Mom asks us.

I look at my watch. It's almost lunchtime.

"Let's set up close to where the food trucks are selling lunch," I say.

Lander and I park the wagon near the food trucks.

"Customers buy products when they're neat, clean, and organized," Mom says.

We gently display ten bouquets. We store the other ten underneath the wagon. Lander sets up our sign.

People line up for lunch. They admire our bouquets. Then, a lady hands me a $5 bill—our first sale!

The lunch line grows longer. We start to sell a lot of our bouquets!

"Bea!" hollers Lander. "Can you grab some more flowers? We're running low again!"

I reach under the wagon. I don't feel any bouquets. I peek under the wagon. I see nothing.

"We sold all the bouquets!" I shout back.

"All of them?!" questions Lander.

"I guess we'll bring more inventory next time!" I say.

"I can't wait to tell Nigel that," Lander replies.

We throw each other a high-five and head home.

Back at my house, Lander and I stack the money we earned onto the counter.

Lander separates the ones and fives into two different piles. Then, I count all the money—$100!

We divide the money evenly. Lander keeps half. I keep half. Fifty dollars for each of us!

Lander and I pinky promise. We will each donate $5 to the local animal shelter.

Hamilton happily wags his tail.

"Thanks for helping me, Bea," Lander says. He turns to leave. "Oh, and, Bea, you were brave to stand up to Nigel."

"Thanks, Lander," I say, nodding.

Lander walks out the door.

"Mom!" I shout, walking into the kitchen.

"Yes, Bea?" Mom answers.

"I liked helping Lander today! It was fun to work together to start a new business. And I made some money!"

"Business can be fun, can't it?" Mom says with a smile. I tap the toe of my shoe. I'm brainstorming again.

Then, a million-dollar idea hits me!
"Mom!" I shout.

"Yes, Bea?" Mom replies.

"Anytime my friends need help with an idea, I want to work with them to create a solution. It could be my own business!"

"Jackpot!" says Mom. "Go for it, Bea!"

Think of yourself as on the threshold of unparalleled success. A whole, clear, glorious life lies before you. Achieve! Achieve!

Andrew Carnegie

First, I need a place to work. My drawing table is the perfect desk. I push it next to Mom's desk.

Also, I will need supplies. I sit down and make a list. Mom and I talk about how I will invest a portion of the $50 I earned today to buy everything I need.

Suddenly, Grandpa's messenger bag from Europe catches my eye. He sent it to me to play dress up. I will use that to hold my supplies!

I tuck my list inside Grandpa's bag.

"Bea is for Business," I say out loud.

I am officially in business!

I know you have great ideas.
I want to help you with them.
Write me!

40430889R00023

Made in the USA
Middletown, DE
12 February 2017